MY REASON

Finds

ISBN: 978-1-63308-277-9 Print

Interior and Cover Design by *R'tor John D. Maghuyop*

CHALFANT ECKERT
PUBLISHING

1028 S Bishop Avenue, Dept. 178
Rolla, MO 65401
Printed in United States of America

MY REASON

Finds

DAD'S POETRY ALIVE

THOMAS DANIEL TRIPLETT, SR.
Compiled by: Felicity Triplett

CHALFANT ECKERT

PUBLISHING

Table of Contents

In Loving Memory
of
Thomas Daniel Triplett
(Dad)

"And so, after he had patiently endured, he obtained the promise."

Hebrews 6:15

The Best

God saw he was getting tired
And a cure was not to be.
So He put His arms around him
And whispered, "Come with Me."

With tearful eyes we watched him
suffer
And saw him fade away.
Although we loved him dearly,
We could not make him stay.

A golden heart stopped beating,
Hard working hands to rest.
God broke our hearts to prove to us
He only takes the best.

Thomas Daniel Triplett

Born
April 1, 1960
St. Louis, Missouri

Passed Away
December 29, 2014
Rolla, Missouri

Memorial Service
Landmark Baptist Church
Rolla, Missouri
Saturday, January 10, 2015
10:00 a.m.

Officiating
Pastor Darren Myers

Obituary

Thomas Daniel Triplett, Sr., of Rolla, passed away on Monday, Dec. 29 at the age of 54. Tom was born on April 1, 1960 in St. Louis, MO to the late Stephen and Theda Triplett. Preceding him in death were his brother Jeff and his niece Lynne.

Tom is survived by his nine children: Christopher and his wife Melissa, Jackie, Thomas, Hope and her husband Jeremiah, Felicity, Ian and Corbin. Surviving siblings include Steve and his wife Pam, Mike and his wife Gina, Mark and his wife Carol, Brian and his wife Gretchen, Kenny and his wife Judy and sister, Tracy. Tom will also leave behind seven grandchildren: Blake, Dustin, Paige, Austin, Jeremiah, Morgan and Jayden.

Tom will be greatly missed by many more family and friends. There will be an open memorial/service to honor Tom's life on Jan. 10, 2015 from 10 a.m. to 2 p.m. held at the Landmark Baptist Church in Rolla.

Published in The Rolla Daily News from Jan. 7 to Jan. 8, 2015 Published in The Rolla Daily News on Jan. 8, 2015- See more at: http://www.legacy.com/obituaries/therolladailynews/obituary.aspx?pid=173761913#sthash.ivhyGGYm.dpuf

Webster University Graduation

Graduate candidates from Webster University's Fort Leonard Wood and Rolla Metropolitan campuses were honored as part of the Fort Leonard Wood Truman Education Center 28th annual combined college graduation ceremony held Oct. 5.

By Staff Reports

Graduate candidates from Webster University's Fort Leonard Wood and Rolla Metropolitan campuses were honored as part of the Fort Leonard Wood Truman Education Center 28th annual combined college graduation ceremony held Oct. 5.

Brig. Gen. Mike Callan (U.S. Air Force, retired), Webster's associate vice president for military and government programs, attended to confer degrees to Webster's graduate degree candidates as part of the ceremony.

Aaron Williams, director of the Fort Leonard Wood Campus, and Felisha Richards, assistant director of the Rolla Metropolitan Campus, assisted Callan as he conferred graduate degrees to 29 Webster students from Fort Leonard Wood and Rolla.

"It was a pleasure to join our recent graduates at Fort Leonard Wood and celebrate their academic achievements," Callan said.

The Webster University Rolla Metropolitan Campus would like to congratulate the following students on graduating with their master's degree:

Andrea Bell, Beth Geoit, Rebecca Lewis, **Thomas Triplett**, Dana Wilson, Autumn Wofford, Elizabeth Cady, Mary Goslin, Angela Chamberlain, Candee Simcox, Vera Cumberland, Cathy Flynt, Julie Boulware, Jason Tonks, Belinda Timm, Stephen Terranova, Betty Baxter, James Goggin, Jamie Bullock, Theresa McDonald, **Amanda Triplett**, Genevieve Doyle, Stephanie Dautenhahn, Arti Dautenhahn, Jason Gramling, Robert Davis, Jeanne Jordon, Amber Walton, Patricia O'Neal-Mellon, Samantha Harris and Denise Dickens.

MY REASON FINDS

What will or will not rob me of my reason?
Does my being bound me to a struggle to survive?
Man has conquered every climate, land, and season.
Is it not yet time for freedom to arrive?

My reason finds this land of milk and honey
is but a land of curd and sour cream.
O'er the ramparts they are looking at us funny
And we are living in a dizzy dream.

Equality and justice were to rid us of despair;
A realm to be the land of the free and the home of the brave.
My reason finds that people are not treated fair
and millions cower in society depraved.

So little honor, truth, or dignity to see
in the people who control the public trust.
My reason finds them representing you and me
the way that bread and butter represent a crust.

Does liberty exist when bound in ropes and chains?
The truth survives by roaming homeless here
and honor is the hunger feeding on our brains.
My reason finds that dignity is fear.

What right is law that lives in economic woe?
What scale of justice makes us rich or poor?
The poor create the riches everywhere to show.
My reason finds them dying to give more.

I say the kings and nobles look us in the face
and we are blinded by the rocket's red glare.
At points my mind will venture slowly into space.
My reason is the bomb that's bursting in the air.

I want my portion of the pie my labors make,
and every man to have their voice be heard.
My reason finds the huddled masses in a lake
and profit merchants call them absurd.

Our leaders have no bearing to determine course
and right or wrong confound the smallest mind.
A storm cloud will not head to threat of brutal force
and reason holds it cannot be confined.

We found our land by questing to be free;
A battered people wanting no more rule.
It was vowed that we would have democracy
And reason finds us going back to school.

THOMAS DANIEL TRIPLETT, SR.

DEEP INSIDE THE MAZE

The witch of old did sear and twist
for having knowledge we had missed.
The citadels of yore but crumbled rock and dirt
for guarding what so causes men to hurt.

Hunger and disease have fed upon the bones
of grievous wretches howling unheard moans.
Our time on earth has been of war and death
because we seek to prove the supremacy of breath.

The rising tide is but our boiling blood
and all dominions vanish in the flood.
Man's partaking lofty tricks and lies
circles to a time when everyone dies.

Religious fiction haunts our nights and days
and keeps us shackled deep inside the maze.
Our struggle is to get into the open air
beyond the walls that trap us in despair.

We need connecting in our minds as men
and go no more to where this God has been.
We must ourselves have honor in our deeds
and be as brothers caring to our needs.

Religion lives, in truth, because we fear.
Yet nothing that it offers us is clear.
What vicious beast devours all our pleasure
and robs a mighty kingdom all its treasure?

Let no doubt stand to question moral right;
There is a light before us shining bright.
A universal force is calling out our name
and God is not player in the game.

Our history is stalking everything we do
and dripping on us like morning dew.
its repetition finds us on the precipice of doom
and we are herding fast unto the plume.

Behold the wisdom we have come to know
to command the chains to let us go.
Defy the gods and vanquish them the maze;
People holding hands and giving praise.

As brothers dare to look death in the face
and take a path about a better place.
Shed the guilt and sorrow of your being
Long enough to look at what you are seeing.

What force might give us what we are
exists on every planet, moon, and start.
The force the same the maze did use
to keep us blind and most confused.

What forms the genes that make us men
is everywhere that space and time have been.
Creation is unique without a god or plan
and we have found the glory given men.

Leave the maze and view what it has hidden
within yourself adjudge what be forbidden.
Equality and justice are blooming in the field
where liberty and freedom come to be revealed.

The age of reason sees what future lies ahead
and gone the maze that filtered what was said.
Behold the power we as men possess
when to ourselves as brothers we confess.

EONS AGO

Eons ago we lived a life in ships and spheres;
A point we reached through many years.
We traveled the universe, seeking peace on many stars:
Our world destroyed by dreadful wars.

We were met with joy because living was our goal.
They knew we sought to have a planet whole.
We spent centuries huddled down beneath our shame.
And time had come to take our places in the game.

We sought out life to bring its knowledge to our aid.
But the conditions for its sharing never were obeyed.
With its science we discovered more vicious ways to kill.
And somehow started taking life at will.

So they sent us off beyond their space
To cause our troubles in some other place.
They gave us no tools with which we could exist.
Because with tools our evil would persist.

Through the ages they thought our knowledge would not hold;
But we have lived, our story was so bold.
We had no materials with which to make our knowledge last.
But it wouldn't vanish with the past.

Our sciences are coming back to mind.
And this sort of puts them in a bind;
To them we are a danger to their star,
Though we remember nothing of the war.

They watch us close to see what we will do.
If we mean death, they want a clue.
If indeed we want a war,
They must disintegrate this star.

There are no chances left to give;
No more free space left to live.
There are no more questions as to why;
There is just but to live or die.

SO UNREAL

So many times I write words not realizing what they say.
Not trying to read them in another way.
They're not always interpreted the way they're meant,
And rarely convey the message that's been sent.

I always try to write the way I feel,
But many times it all seems so unreal.
Many times I figure that which must be said,
Only to misplace the thoughts inside my head.

I can begin a simple line of thought.
But in the end it comes to naught.
Now, for instance, I can think of nothing else to say,
So I will approach you in another way.

It seems I back into a corner leaving no way out,
Left to stand there none too stout.
All so often knowing nothing else to try.
Alone I stare into the sky.

Through the years my mind has gathered slack.
And the tension isn't coming back.
Thinking all my thoughts have doubled,
I find myself often troubled.

I guess being older clears a lot of thoughts to see,
Because the more I age the less I feel free.
More and more there are ends for making meet,
And even when I have the battle won I'm beat.

PERHAPS ONE DAY

I am not stupid, none can say,
Unless it be to their dismay.
Maybe I don't always hold myself in check,
But what the heck?

Many people think of life as torrid,
And never understand what makes it horrid.
I've no concern for social stance,
So I can relax when I have the chance.

Death, to me, just comes and goes;
Why it happens none knows.
You struggle for a final breath to take.
But not one difference will it make.

A lot of people think that God is here.
But do not listen when they hear.
A brighter man is always born
When intelligence dies in scorn.

As scientists probe into the mind,
They'll find the truth is there to find.
Mankind will truly soar the skies
When the power of thought is helped to rise.

The Bible says richness comes to man,
And I believe, because I can.
We launch our spaceships for the stars,
And one day they will be as common as our cars.

God grants life and death, and cures the lame,
But don't our doctors seek to do the same?
God can tumble mountains and drain the seas,
But man is also doing these.

God roams the world changing human ways,
But man does too these days.
Man, himself, still strives for peace;
Even the insane want hate to cease.

I'm telling you that man is smart;
Look ahead and have a heart.
We discover miracles all so fast,
Each one better than the last.

Regeneration keeps life going fine,
So death itself is a living mine.
All life returns from whence it came,
And death renews it just the same.

This life is just to get you set
For the one that's coming yet,
So you should always try your best;
Maybe in the next one you'll have rest.

Why should you spend your time in toil
When life itself was to be royal?
Open your mind for other folks to view,
And perhaps one day they'll share theirs too.

If there's a goal you must achieve,
Then it's one that only you conceive.
Your intelligence will go unknown
If you try having it alone.

It really doesn't matter how smart you are;
Death will strike both near and far.
It does no good to combat death
When it alone can give you breath.

Don't ever think you'll not amount to anything,
Because you do not need a voice to sing.
You see, your mind commands our soul,
Even well beyond the hole.

Death has life to confiscate;
Death has life to reinstate.
Your self does not deactivate,
But death will not negotiate.

This life's thoughts are stored away
For reference in another day.
Keep adding to the experience that you've got,
So that every moment will be caught.

I'VE ENVISIONED THE NEED

I've envisioned the need whereby man came upon this earth;
Reaching within myself I find the knowledge that man is here to prove his worth.
We've poisoned the water, corrupted the land, and polluted the air we need to breathe;
Still we breed and interact as though our time will never leave.

There was a dream that a being could be created which would know no thing but love;
The heart of a lion, but gentle as a dove.
This was man in what was first of all intended,
But through our sin this function was rescinded.

GHASTLY DEVASTATION

There are methods by which the mind will pull upon the self,
as the mind controls the things that we conceive as real.
The ego, having life, is looked upon as provider of our health;
However, it is mind that seeks the strengths we see and feel.

The mind was here as essence long before the body got its form,
and it alone will hear the people mourn.
Our bodies spiral off as if in resignation,
but the mind will last beyond the ghastly devastation.

THOMAS DANIEL TRIPLETT, SR.

I AM HERE

Apart from you I cannot ever sleep;
I see your pain and can but weep.
Your every motion I can see;
I know you are not free.

I want to take your hand and hold you close to me;
To open your eyes to the world and all there is to see;
To give you tranquility far beyond compare;
To make you know within your heart how much I care.

I love you so, and yet we go two different ways;
Your world is one of plays.
I'd like to be a righteous man,
But I think you have another plan.

You say you love me, as though a thought could make me smile;
Your sincerity only lasts the smallest while.
I sit here alone, deserted, sadness in my heart;
I have watched you tear your planet all apart.

You tell me things that only make me cry,
Torture me each time a day goes by.
You say you love me, but it really is quite rude;
I think that all your actions make the statement lewd.

You do the things I never thought you would,
Committed sins every time you thought you could.
I watch you try to justify your pain.
And I wonder if I really made you sane.

I remain silent because there are no excuses I can give,
But I cannot let this evil live.
You interpret this as though I somehow hide the truth,
But I told you at the start that there would be no proof.

THE EAGLE IS A FREE THING

The eagle is a free thing;
a bird that gets around.
It makes my heart and mind both sing
to watch it soar above the ground.

Much too smart to ever blunder;
A bird that flies with ease.
Indeed it is a wonder
to anyone who sees.

It's something you can look at;
Something to be proud of.
It holds its wings both wide and flat;
No need to push and shove.

A man could never be this free;
But only if he could.
Life could be the same, you see;
only if it would.

THOMAS DANIEL TRIPLETT, SR.

A FATE MORE AWESOME

He walked the land for naught but good,
And spread his love to all he could
He wept for all our windswept souls,
And taught us of his dream-like goals.

The mean he trusted were quite few;
Their auras were a different hue.
A million faces, twelve small men;
A sea of darkness called our sin.

Persecuted for his words of peace,
He said our torment wouldn't cease.
He understood both large and small,
Though heeded nothing but the call.

Over deserts, swollen feet;
Small oasis, awesome heat.
Mountaintops and valley floors;
At our markets, at our doors.

Twelve men guided by a light,
Casting shadows in the night;
Men unshaken in their dream,
And no erosion from the stream.

He cried he knew the evil in our blood;
He saw a fate more awesome than the flood;
Annihilation of the human race;
His brothers blasted out of space.

Those surviving will not ever ease their pain;
Their skin devoured by the rain.
They search out comfort, none is near;
They plead for mercy, none can hear.

Molten rock and burning trees;
Poisons thriving in the breeze.
Cities leveled to the ground;
There is no shelter to be found.

Time will pass with men reverting back to apes.
Chipping stones and carving shapes;
Tribes are formed for hunting meals,
And laws are made for one who steals.

Over deserts, swollen feet;
Small oasis, awesome heat.
Mountaintops and valley floors;
At our markets, at our doors.

OVERWHELMING ECSTASY

I had a dream, though quite unlike the others I have had;
I was so overwhelmed with joy that it made me feel had.
A dream, I know, and yet it had a different air;
It was as if somehow I really was right there.

I traveled down a hallway quite well worn in years,
And yet I knew inside it was constructed by my peers.
The lanes were overgrown with shrubs and weeds.
As if their time had passed to serve our needs.

I was searching for a grave I knew not where to find,
And I was neither sure of purpose in my mind.
I found the grave, but there was more than one;
I thought that there was surely something funny going on.

The date of birth left nothing to decide,
But each one differed from the day the person died.
I pondered for a moment just what this could mean,
And in a flash I came upon another scene.

A woman came and told me what it was I sought;
It was, in fact, the lessons that were taught.
She told me in the grave there was a book,
And I must leave at once to have another look.

I came upon a castle wholly unawares;
A monk that wanted me to climb some stairs.
Perhaps it was the way he merely stood and pointed,
But something made me wonder how he came to be anointed.

Another handed me a chain of gold of senseless length,
With which I struck the first with all my strength.
He simply disappeared, as though he had never been there.
I paused for one brief moment, just to stare.

The other draped more chains around his neck,
And then he glanced at me to check.
In his eyes I guess I saw that everything was fine,
Because we climbed the stairs in line.

I followed through a dark-enshrouded hall,
Wondering why I had to heed his call.
He opened a door, and all of time did cease;
I was at once aware of inner peace.

In the middle of the room there was a monk who held a book;
A Bible, with that really antiquated look.
It was black, with a cross designed in gold;
The truth of eons written in its fold.

As he opened it, it seemed the earth was new;
Nothing else had ever struck me as so true.
I felt a breeze, but all the wind was gone.
I knew that God was here, and this was dawn.

The curtains billowed in a wind that simply wasn't there;
I felt relieved of every earthly care.
So much pressure offered nothing to resent;
I felt it urgent to repent.

I flung myself upon a bed, and tears came flooding to my eyes.
I cried from joy that God was now beneath our skies.
No tears of pain, just glee and overwhelming joy;
Begging forgiveness, as if I were a little boy.

I felt a love I could not turn away,
And I knew that Jesus had returned to stay.
I cried, but merriment was in my soul;
I was not distressed to pay the toll.

My Lord is here! This knowledge felt so good.
I repented, as I also think you should.
Overwhelming ecstasy for incomparable pleasure;
Perhaps a dream, but in it was a way of life; a treasure.

CAN YOU PEOPLE
NOT OBSERVE?

Can you people not observe the passage of a day?
Can you not see that God will have the final say?
Realize, my friends, that we are near the end of time;
God is coming, and you will burn for all your crime.

God was enraged when Eve had Adam eat the fruit,
Because in that instant, the sin of doubt was given root.
It expanded in proportion, until all of life was in the dark.
Incensed enough to flood the earth, except for Noah and his Ark.

Thus Noah started life anew for each and every man,
But sin returned to spread across the land.
So God dispatched His only son to cleanse our souls of wrong.
He was murdered by the throng.

Can you people not observe the passage of a day?
Can you not see that God will have the final say?
You slew His son, but not the Word he preached;
In the end you will repent for this promise that was breached.

He keeps providing selfless love for all,
Yet you persist to live beyond His call.
You keep on loving life for the stories you can tell;
Seldom do you stop to think that He will have you roast in Hell.

Realize, my friend, that Satan can in no way win this war;
God will grab his horns and stuff him in a jar.
Please, heed the calling from above;
Do not again reject His love.

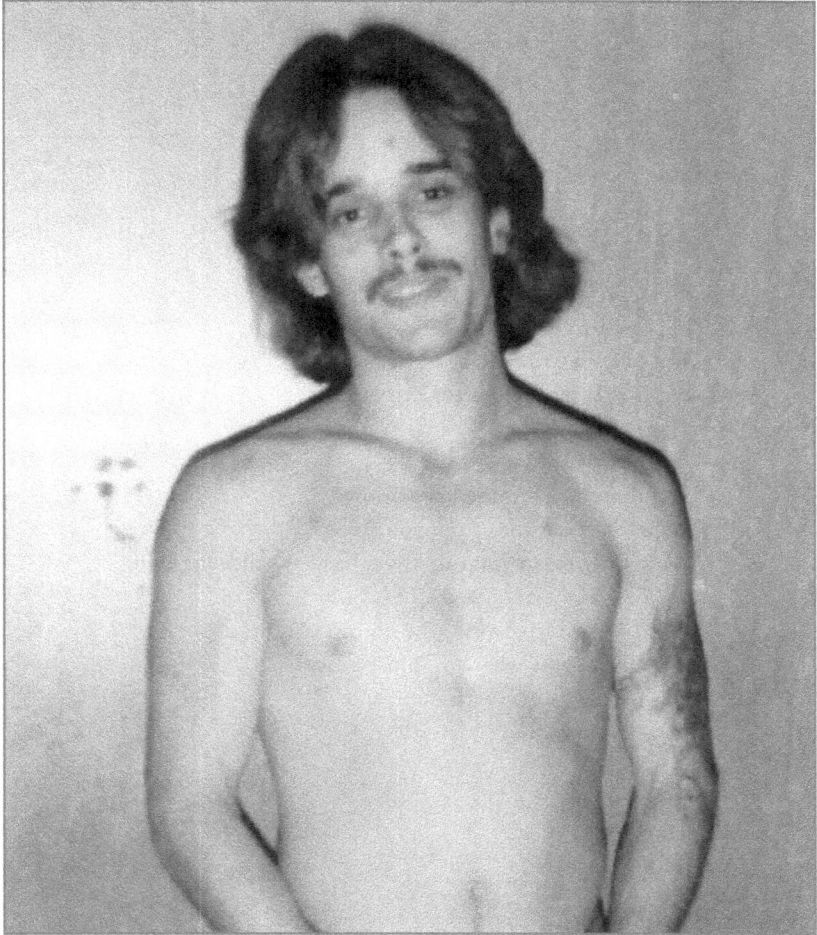

I CAN'T SEE

I've so much love to give to you
but it seems you won't believe it's true.
You've ample time to curse at me,
but that is more than anger that I see.

You never try to check the flow,
as if there's something kept below.
Such foul emissions from your tongue
could only mean you think you have me chewing dung.

I find it hard to get into the groove
when I can't see what you must prove.
You are not at war with me;
Why can't you see?

IF I VENTURE

Captivated by your wit and charm,
caught by the simplicity of thought.
I wonder if my heart will come to harm
if I venture past the things I sought.

What is here once was not there,
and what was sure now is not clear.
A friend indeed, and one to care;
One to listen who can hear.

You really mean the world to me,
but I do so fear to let you know.
I fear that if I let you see,
you will turn your head and go.

TO HAVE THEIR VISION SEEN

This species here on earth is bent, it seems, on exploring beyond their sphere.
For centuries now they've sought those truths which caused their life to be.
Today they seek the wisdom of the ancients and somehow hope to see it clear;
Humans reach for the stars through ignorance as they flounder on their sea.

They're gaining knowledge from the substance which they've barely chipped away.
And an understanding comes about that what is now beneath their seas was
once a dry and fertile land.
Places like Atlantis are fast becoming known to have truly existed for a day,
And there is something awry in the way these mighty nations sank beneath the sand.

They haven't gained the wisdom that it takes to have their vision seen;
The primitive way of man on earth must be eradicated before some glory comes to light.
The beast that dwells within man's soul has made his prospects very lean;
Even while their leaders talk of peace, they have but malice in their sight.

CAN YOU TELL ME?

Can you tell me why I find it necessary to cope with the life you present to me?
What necessity could cause me to create a delusion with which I cannot find
the time to live?
It seems so distant, the time and place in which my mind began to grasp the sea;
Perhaps the time was waned when I so freely felt the things I had to give.

You speak of love, but love is trust and you just give me none to feel.
Nature itself is love, and never should a person try to keep it as their own.
I don't believe you know the meaning of love, or even sense that it is real;
I can't see how that which is responsible could be determined by you alone.

If we cannot get along together, it makes no sense to me why we should stay.
I view this family as if it were mine, and no other way will ever come to be;
You can have whatever game you have a need yourself to play,
It's not for me.

THOMAS DANIEL TRIPLETT, SR.

TURNING POINT

I sit here now as if I'm broken,
searching my mind for some small token.
The best I had just would not last,
another item in my past.
I search quite hard but still can't find
a reason in my mind.

I've no assurance that you are there;
no real knowledge that you may care.
You neglect to give me what I need,
no matter how I beg and plead.
I need you more since I'm in here,
for reasons all quite clear.

The loneliness I feel inside this cage
brings in me a burning rage,
because all the friends I had while free
couldn't now care less at all for me.
They thought I was a friendly guy
while I was there and getting high.

I'll blame no soul for what I lose;
I led my life, and I did choose.
It doesn't matter that I've gone away,
I am me every day.
I take the blame for what I fail;
I am fault inside this jail.

A BUBBLE BOUND
TO BURST

Shaded alleys have no light,
and crimes of passion have no heart.
A blind man never sees a sight,
but he's in life to be a part.

A broken wing will never let you fly,
and twisted legs will never let you walk.
Eagles soar across the sky,
and deaf mutes find it hard to talk.

A clock cannot run without a gear,
and buffalo starve without the range;
A bold man seldom ever sheds a tear,
and life will never change.

A problem mounts into a war,
and misconceptions plague the mind.
A rocket launched to reach a star,
and none knows what it will find.

A glass of sand can no way quench a thirst,
and gravel cannot make a meal;
A dream is a bubble bound to burst
and leave a man with naught to feel.

Veins of ice can never make you warm;
and shattered nerves will put you in a grave;
Passion brings you no more harm,
and never worries what is brave.

BEYOND THE HILL

Standing amidst a mountain stream
gazing at the crests beyond the hill,
I swell my chest to scream
A resonant sound designed to kill.

Enunciations go unheeded in the night;
Dreams of all this perpetrated death.
I'll shore some ground to stem the flight,
But I doubt if I can save your breath.

WE HESITATE TO SOAR

The stars are numbered many;
but speckles up above
If ever stand on any
is more than I can think of.

Billions of miles a man could go
to tame demented races.
We could show them how to grow
if we would dwell upon their graces.

Nine planets in our solar system,
and our galaxy has stars galore,
Yet with all our wisdom
we hesitate to soar.

We fight in wars that we detest,
when we know of better things to do.
We make our pledges to protest,
but seldom ever follow through.

For me, much education is needed
to attain the goal for which I reach,
but I'm constantly impeded
by those who have a need to preach.

I would teach of distant stars,
and of the many things I've seen.
I would teach you folks that wars
are dirty, cruel and mean.

Some would say I rant and rave
about things I could not know,
but I'll go to my grave
before their truths will grow.

The victory wouldn't be an easy one,
but nor are any others.
At least when I am dead and gone
the truth will live inside my brothers.

THE SEVENTH DAY

Let theologians say what they must say,
the Lord could not have rested on the seventh day.
He had to duplicate the sun that shined
to make the beauty of your kind.

To make you a star in a world of ghouls,
He had to set aside the rules.
in your making He did everything He could;
Your splendor shows that God is good.

In your being He embedded every season;
it must have taken weeks to simplify the reason.
Evil was forgotten when the good Lord gave you birth,
to ensure that you survive this dreadful earth.

A hear that's filled to overflowing with His love,
and eyes so blue to sparkle with the skies above.
In you the wonders never ceased;
Your living will most surely slay the beast.

WHAT INDEED?

Mysteries existent in a dream;
Are things really what they seem?
Disregarded acts of fate;
What have we become of late?

Death is where it may begin,
but who are we to start again?
Man himself is the redundance,
Life was given in abundance.

When we still die in petty wars,
Who are we to search the stars?
If we can't find some love and live,
what indeed have we to give?

Who would have us share their skies;
Who would want our hate and lies?
Restricted thus the way we fight,
we may not ever see the light.

A CAT

A powerful animal is the cat,
Still proud and running free.
I take pleasure in the fact
That such a thing can be.

They exist in a life so humble,
Quite content to not be man.
Only when hungry will they grumble,
Taking comfort when they can.

I would like to have one for my own,
To raise with loving care.
I know when it was gown
My den would be its lair.

A Cheetah is the best, I'd say,
For they run pretty strong.
If I'd befriend one in m day,
The fact would be a song.

I know it would protect me,
And I would take it out to hunt.
If my quarry thought to flee,
Then I would only need to grunt.

A friendship with a pet will last
Much longer than you know.
It is of another case,
And always there to show.

You must show one that you care,
But it isn't hard to do;
Just take with you everywhere,
And keep it well fed too.

To some people it may seem
That this idea is crazy,
But hey could never dream
Of a pet that isn't lazy.

Indeed there are some creatures
That may make better pets,
But the sleekness of a Cheetah's features
Is where I'd place my bets.

HE SAYS

"Grab my hand," He says, "and I will show you peace.
Follow me if you want wars to cease.
Gracious meadows bending in a breeze;
Birds of splendor in the trees.

Gushing streams, babbling brooks;
Life of richness, no more crooks.
A man need never fear to show his love;
When all is plenty, who would shove?

Cloths? Indeed; the finest silks.
Never liquor, never milk.
For your meals you need never strain;
You'll have no need for meat or grain.

The peace inside your heart is mine.
So tell me if it feels fine.
Life is granted up until you die.
But we can manage, you and I.

Alone, your life is but a ghoulish dream;
Left to sizzle while you scream.
Alone, you'll always have depression near;
Left to cringe in quaking fear."

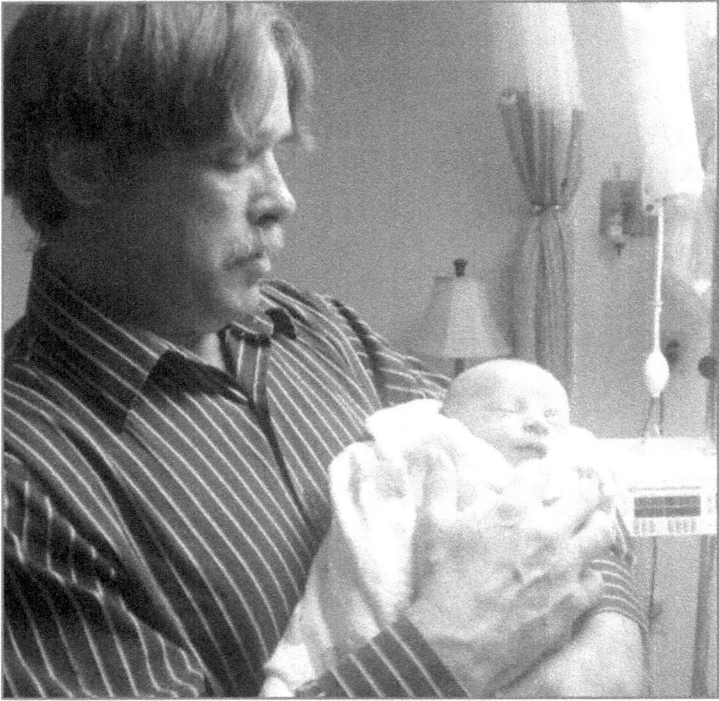

THERE IS A POINT

There is a point where a focus comes to mind,
a single passage through the maze.
A source is never really hard to find,
a single message through the days.

We are naught but shadows of the sun,
merely mist dispersing with the time.
A wave of people on the run;
A death watch in its prime.

THOMAS DANIEL TRIPLETT, SR.

ALL AROUND ME

All around me, torn and aimless souls;
Unnecessary, unneeded, unattainable goals.
Struggles for things not useful for existence;
Offering up to pleasure but resistance.

All around me, men perplexed with mystery;
Seeking escape by refusing to see their history.
Waging wars to prove their cause,
never seeing their own flaws.

All around me, fascination with physical might;
Forever evading the call to what is right,
Continually denying that violence is their aim,
they plot their course to win the game.

All around me, life destroyed; starvation, death;
Peace existing only in some final breath.
Over the world, men will die in rags,
and the rich man packs his many bags.

All around me, greed is seething on the earth,
erasing the wonder of our birth.
Men talk of peace, knowing that words won't do;
They aim their guns at me and you.

All around me, children begging us to learn;
They know that at this pace we're sure to burn.
Children see the world and want to reach,
not understanding what these madmen preach.

All around me, children look to find a way,
but none cares what they might say.
They reach so desperately to find a reason,
only to be silenced by talk of treason.

All around me, knowledge wasted; none has the ears.
They say they'll gain it in their years.
Never admitting they're playing possum,
they claim that time will see peace blossom.

All around me, a sadly civilized race;
Not one person looking another in the face,
not one person seeking out another mind
for the joy involved through life combined.

THOMAS DANIEL TRIPLETT, SR.

PROVIDE THE KNOWLEDGE

A metamorphosis occurs when people think;
Neural wavelengths forming patterns as they link.
The revelations found existent in a dream
provide the knowledge with which we feed the stream.

Quite elusive are the workings of the brain;
Extensive askance has yet to life the strain.
Minds will snap if questions run too deep,
leaving one a gnarled, crumbled heap.

Defeat, you see, is awaiting those who win,
because they've naught to do but start again.
Thoughts are good, but often do not lead,
as proven by millions left in need.

MOVE ON

What can you do
when you've done all else?
It's sad but it's true
how there seems nothing else.

How long can you wonder?
How long can you think?
How much will you blunder
in a blink?

When will they see
that I'm already gone?
Just let me be,
so I can move on.

THOMAS DANIEL TRIPLETT, SR.

MUST WE MISS?

What do you do when the well runs dry?
Where do you run when you want to cry?
How do you touch the clouds above the plain?
The earth is large, or I'm insane.

Who among our human race
can say we're not from outer space?
Who among us here on earth
can state the origin of our birth?

How intelligent are our minds
when placed beside genetic finds?
How long must we hover in suspense
before our being makes some sense?

How long must we miss the ones we love
before we cease to push and shove?
It won't be long before we leave,
But eternity is next, I grieve.

How many people today are threatened
by the power of our peaceful weapons?
If we're so smart, then why do we persist
when all the logic says desist?

MISERY

Misery is a word
that's been around a while
so is it absurd
to greet it with a smile?

I tell you with my heart
that misery may be needed,
so if you're really smart
don't thing you've been defeated.

Misery comes to every man,
but it always goes away.
Do the best with what you can;
Tomorrow is another day.

Misery is infection,
but there really is a cure;
Give it some inspection
and it is gone for sure.

Misery is a word
that's been around a while,
and it may be absurd,
but in the end it lets you smile.

THOMAS DANIEL TRIPLETT, SR.

ANOTHER SPACE

I've got to write these lines of wit,
and make the words as I see fit.
Perhaps there is no point to hit,
but that doesn't bother me a bit.

Now over yonder there's a cold dark pit,
and over this pit you cannot sit.
It goes down deep and isn't lit;
The sides are rough and lined with grit.

I want to turn around and flee;
This here pit seems bad to me.
I think it's reared my curiosity,
this pit without a door or key.

If I enter what is there to see?
it makes it just a bit eerie.
It's hard to say what is to be;
No sense in giving the third degree.

If the truth may seem a bit too raw,
it is the truth without a flaw;
I went in and what I saw
made me stand and gaze in awe.

The man inside was twelve feet tall,
and he insisted that I brawl.
I told him I must take another call;
He was much too big for me to fall.

Then he approached me where I sat,
and said he simply had to chat.
I knew not what to say to that;
He smelled so like an evil rat.

He said there were some words he lacked,
but that had to share a fact;
He said the way in which we humans act
is sure to leave our bodies stacked.

He led me all about the place
with visions of the human race.
He spoke as though a demon had his face;
I thought to seek another space.

I listened to everything he had to say
because I could not turn away.
At one he spoke of how we play,
and showed me sights of how we slay.

It ripped my heart to see the joy inside this guy,
and even more when he said why;
He said that everyone beneath the sky
would go to him when humans die.

With that I lunged to pluck out his one eye,
and he knocked me down with but a sigh.
He said he knew that I would try
because the truth is much too dry.

Then there was an awful rumble of the ground,
and I saw the big man sat and bound.
I looked, and none else was near around;
I hadn't even heard a sound.

 A flash occurred and the surf did pound;
Another Queen of England crowned.
The guy, I know, was twelve feet tall and round;
Stranger things on earth abound.

I never saw his face again,
but if I see a pit I won't go in;
It's enough to think and remember when.
Let our little world spin.

Of what I saw, I dare not tell a friend;
Truth and terror make an awful blend.
To let them think that all of life is but a trend
is the best there is to offer in the end.

REACH OUT YOUR HAND

There is a mountain over there, reach out your hand;
Beyond it lies the richest land.
Dreams blossom into flowers in those soils;
Happiness where anger never boils.

The ground itself is pure and clean;
Vegetation grows to be the darkest green.
Your simple presence pays the fare;
There lurks no danger in the air.

Millions desire to make the trip, but I have chosen you;
Your eyes see life in quite a different view.
Your thoughts and dreams that wars should cease
make you welcome in our place of peace.

All rivers and streams are crystal clear;
You'll find no trace of drugs or beer.
The skies so clean, so blue, so bright;
There are no teardrops in the night.

There is a mountain over there, reach out your hand;
Beyond it lies the richest land.
Climb the mountain, I will set the table;
The land of Eden was no fable.

SOMETHING THERE

A thought is something there I cannot feel;
A sense I can't dismiss because it's real.
Something in the dark demanding light;
Advancing, yet its shadow hinders sight.

Possessing rhythm, yet devoid of tones;
Something gnawing at the marrow of my bones.
Something that I think pursues my very soul,
although destruction doesn't seem to be its goal.

It's there; approaching, causing changes in the air.
It's as though my being were its lair.
Concentration very closely gives it shape,
Yet no dimension; always they escape.

Coming closer; with each moment does it gain.
I'd feel threatened, but it offers me no pain.
A power much more awesome than I know;
A gentle ease with which I sense this terror grow.

Creating thoughts that flow forth in a stream;
A presence gaining resurrection in a dream.
Nearing ever more and still not there to see;
What is this thing that puzzles me?

THOMAS DANIEL TRIPLETT, SR.

LIFE

Life is beautiful,
and most people love it,
but it may be fatal;
It's what you make of it.

You grow from youth,
and you think you're smart;
You think your thoughts are truth,
but they really aren't.

You ask your dad for money;
You just assume he's rich.
You think that sounds funny,
but you think your mom's a witch.

Then you're in your teens;
You think your dad's a nut.
You think up all your schemes
to find the corners that you cut.

Now you want a car,
and you're not really joking,
But I'm afraid you're off by far,
because finances have you choking.

Your dad right now is mad,
because he has been robbed.
You know indeed this does sound bad,
but he also lost his job.

So now that you are married,
speaking for adults,
reflect on how you tarried
and curse not what you sulk.

Now your parents are dead and gone;
You can no longer blame them.
Left here so to carry on,
your mind all numb and dim.

Now that you have grown,
and learned a thing or two,
you find it has been shown
your folks were not so dumb as you.

You sit and think of times gone by,
of days grown very old;
So many things you had to try
to prove that you were bold.

Now you are well upon an age
when all your kinfolk turn to fools;
They know that you are near the stage
when they can split up all your jewels.

All those friends that you had made
are still your friends to call,
but you've belongings they can raid
if you'd just finally fall.

The time has come and you are dead;
Indeed you've really grown.
You have a gravestone at your head,
and a place to call your own.

FAINTLY ECHOED
IN THE NIGHT

A message faintly echoed in the night;
urgent whispers telling me to write.
An image just appears in sigh
when it fades before the light.

The wisdom gathered in my years
is the source of all my fears;
A man who fights to top his peers
is always gone when he appears.

He gains the knowledge that he needs
to stem the thoughts of other creeds.
Before him we are naught but weeks,
and he has got another bag of seeds.

We must have peace and play on earth,
lest we never realize our worth.
We must keep wisdom in our hearth,
lest we cease creating birth.

SENSES

I can touch the street
with my feet;
I can see the skies
with my eyes;
I can feel a part
with my heart;
I can feel the drain
upon my brain;
I can hear quite clear
with my ear;
I can smell out foes
with my nose;
I can grip your charms
with my arms.
I know what I find
on my mind.
I can sense your yen
with my skin,
And I can feel your love
with mine.

THOMAS DANIEL TRIPLETT, SR.

THINGS SO REAL

How can I put words together when I don't know
which way I want my thoughts to go?
With a million things to write about,
it isn't right to leave one out.

I could write of the beauty here on earth,
or the fascination of our birth.
I could write of flowers growing big,
or giant trees we cut to twigs.

I could write of the abundance life was granted,
but that has since been all supplanted.
I could teach you things so real;
I could make your heart jump out and feel.

I could make you sad enough to cry
and keep your spirits soaring high.
I would make you feel low,
and show you how that helps you grow.

I don't have to prove I'm strong
by telling you you're wrong,
and I don't have to be too smart
to make you happy in your heart.

I am not right in everything I speak,
but aren't we all a little weak?
I know enough to see me through,
and that's enough to do.

If we were all so damn precise,
who would we entice?
If we were all as smart as we pretend,
with whom would we contend?

You've no word in how I act,
and don't you try explaining tact.
You think you are so awful cool,
but let me note that you're a fool.

I can picture all the times you've lied,
and all the phony tricks you've tried;
Who are you to tell me how to be,
when you yourself don't truly see?

VANQUISH SHADOWS

To have the blessings of your friends
is to have the world by its ends,
so to have the blessings of a foe
is by far a better way to go.

Having someone to hold tight
can vanquish shadows to the light,
and knowing someone you can trust
is like having extra thrust.

Coping with life and all its harm
enables one to grow in charm.
For one who's living it alone,
a path is there but overgrown.

It makes me happy to know I'm here,
that I decide which way to steer.
I wonder who I might inspire
to a goal that's even higher.

Living life the best that I know how
is the least I can allow.
I ponder things for which most don't care,
but I find my comfort there.

I don't care if you don't like the things I do,
but I want you to be happy too.
I like doing things off-the-cuff,
no matter if it makes life rough.

I see sadness once in some great while,
and now and then I lose my smile,
but things are better in another day,
so I just go about my way.

I find interest in the earth, the moon, and the space above.
I'm serious about poker, pool and love.
Things don't always go so right,
but that's no cause to get uptight.

I can't say I never frown,
but there isn't much that gets me down.
With you I've all I ever want or need,
and my emotions won't recede.

THOMAS DANIEL TRIPLETT, SR.

HOW THINGS COULD BE

Sometimes I'm hopping like a hare,
and others I slumber like a bear.
I take to comfort like a beagle,
and I've the spirit of an eagle.

I've the agility of a cat,
and the sonar of a bat.
Given the ferocity of a rabid dog,
I've the patience of a frog.

Mostly tame as a Meadow Lark,
I can be deadly like a shark.
I could tell you things I've heard
from the whisper of a bird.

I've all these creatures locked within me,
as you can plainly see,
but keeping them in proper frame
is not an easy game.

But manage I must do,
with this weird assorted zoo;
An ant will stay inside his border
and live his life in order.

If you hear these words and truly see,
you will know how things could be.
it would give your heart a lift
to know you are a gift.

I wrote these words so long ago,
but they've a meaning I still know;
They've a message to conceal,
but above all else they are so real.

There's pleasure in a dove,
and happiness in love;
There's softness in a fur,
and warm that does concur.

Come with me, I know you still;
You're the air that moves my gill.
You're the wind that gives me flight;
The banishment of blight.

I'm the sheep and you're the shepherd;
I'm the plain and you're the leopard;
I'm the forest and you're the dear;
Do you know what I'm saying here?

NO MATTER WHAT WE YEARN

Since the beginning of time
man has wondered
if it really was a crime
when he blundered.

At first he didn't care,
then his mind began to grow;
He no longer walked bare,
nor wandered to and fro.

He settled down and planted crops
because he had to feed his face.
He built a city full of shops,
and conquered every living space.

We've ventured far since then,
but it isn't over yet;
We look upon ourselves as men,
and war is what we get.

We've learned through time to love,
and yet we have no peace.
Somehow still we push and shove
to find the golden fleece.

THOMAS DANIEL TRIPLETT, SR.

FEELING LOW
JUST NEVER PAYS

Hello there, and how are you;
Feeling low or kind of blue?
I know you don't feel too good these days,
but feeling low just never pays.

To tell you the truth, I don't feel too good either;
I feel I need to take a breather.
I think sometimes of what life means,
and get depressed about the scenes.

I am trying hard to make life good,
and I would do it if I could,
but I've a horrid lot to learn
before I'm sure of what I yearn.

I quit school when I was young;
I got tired of hearing dung.
My instructors did not know how to teach
of the things I had a need to reach.

I've now a past I need to fight,
and sometimes things just don't go right.
Inside I feel a need for school,
but I cannot take a stagnant pool.

I've got to break my habit of being lazy,
and keep my thoughts from being crazy.
There's no need for me to come on strong,
as that leaves one's impressions wrong.

I know at heart just how to act,
but it's hard to follow through exact.
I know just what I want to do,
but not how I'm to see it through.

These words were written so you'd be shown
that you are sad, but not alone.
I know you don't feel too good these days,
but feeling low just never pays.

THOMAS DANIEL TRIPLETT, SR.

OF OUR BREATH

Somewhere on this earth there is a precipice that overlooks the dawn of man;
There lies a message well encoded that will tell us all the basic plan.
Right now we've erred, and as such we've doomed the earth to burn;
But there is yet so much a chance we may have the peace to yearn.

On this sphere we call our home, we men have conquered many plights,
and I contend that we will slay this dragon long before the air ignites.
But we are men who cannot cease our hope by the very nature of our breath,
so we will go on laughing up until our death.

THOSE WHO WANT
TO HAVE A SAY

Man uses his mental forces to create destruction for all who do not see his way,
and spends billions of dollars every year to silence those who want to have a say.
Evil and atrocity exist within the boundaries of this land of milk and honey;
To them this is the way of life, thus somehow your objections all sound funny.
If I were one they thought as real, then perhaps I'd gain a form by which to speak;
I exist beyond the time when all their might has fallen to the meek.

THOMAS DANIEL TRIPLETT, SR.

SIGHT IS MINE

I watch the day flow by with hopeful eyes,
awaiting the moment when I may soar the skies.
I seek the heights that all men wish to gain;
To soar beyond the clouds, bypass the rain.

I've yet to see a mountain too high for me to climb;
awaiting the day when all in sight is mine.
I seek the deepest ocean in which to take a swim;
To dive or float, whatever is my whim.

I see the desert spanning all across my view,
beneath a sky quite cloudless, in color pale blue.
I've had the greenest forests start a throbbing in my heart;
Such awesome beauty, I know not where to start.

The amazement of the sages, a song unto my soul;
An empty furnace now stuffed full of coal.
I've felt you nestle close to me,
and I know how happy I can be.

Your thoughts and dreams are all I hear;
The words you speak are very dear.
I'm truly glad you came into my life
and volunteered to be my wife.

HOW STRANGE LOVE
MUST BE

How strange love must be,
how it comes to every man,
but seldom to me
such as hand in hand.

How strange it must seem;
How people start out
two as a team;
Two beings quite stout.

How strange it may grow
when nothing is sought.
I used to say no,
but now I am caught.

How strange it appears
in the wink of an eye;
How strange it adheres
when you don't even try.

How strange love must be,
how it comes to every man;
It's come unto me,
and I have your hand.

THE STRONGEST

Russia is deceased, but that is not the problem here;
Where is what we once held dear?
Our greatest minds had all sought peace;
They knew this hatred had to cease.

Night has stayed long past the dawn;
Chicago is smashed and St. Louis gone.
They knew their weapons would not set them free,
and yet raced on to World War Three.

Amidst the rubble and ash of what is left,
I can see nothing but the theft;
Millions living life and going their own way,
when a searing flash dismissed the day.

To each horizon there is nothing to be seen;
Nothing moves, and nothing now grows green.
Beyond this even, there are pits where cities were,
and embers where the strongest thought they could endure.

Bodies torn and blistered by the heat;
These are the terms they chose to meet.
Petty quarrels led to mass destruction;
They would not listen to instruction.

All their facts, and nothing lying underneath;
Where is what they promised to bequeath?
Their glory is not even now a dream;
We have no river, lake or stream.

I stand here now for little worth,
and sob for the meek who get this earth.
The proud have left it barren of its life;
Cut away as with a knife.

Just today I talked with friends who cared for me,
and now I've none of them to see.
Our leaders said it would not get this bad,
but where is what we had?

They built those missiles for defense?
I think the truth's much more intense.
They never looked at earth as more than wasted nations;
They merely ordered troops to battle stations.

The trees in Maine are burnt to cinders,
and Detroit is finished making fenders.
Who cares that Russia will not rise again?
Where are all our able men?

Communism slain, but democracy void of people;
Religion lives, but nowhere have I seen a steeple.
Freedom soars, but only in a myth;
What have we to function with?

THOMAS DANIEL TRIPLETT, SR.

73

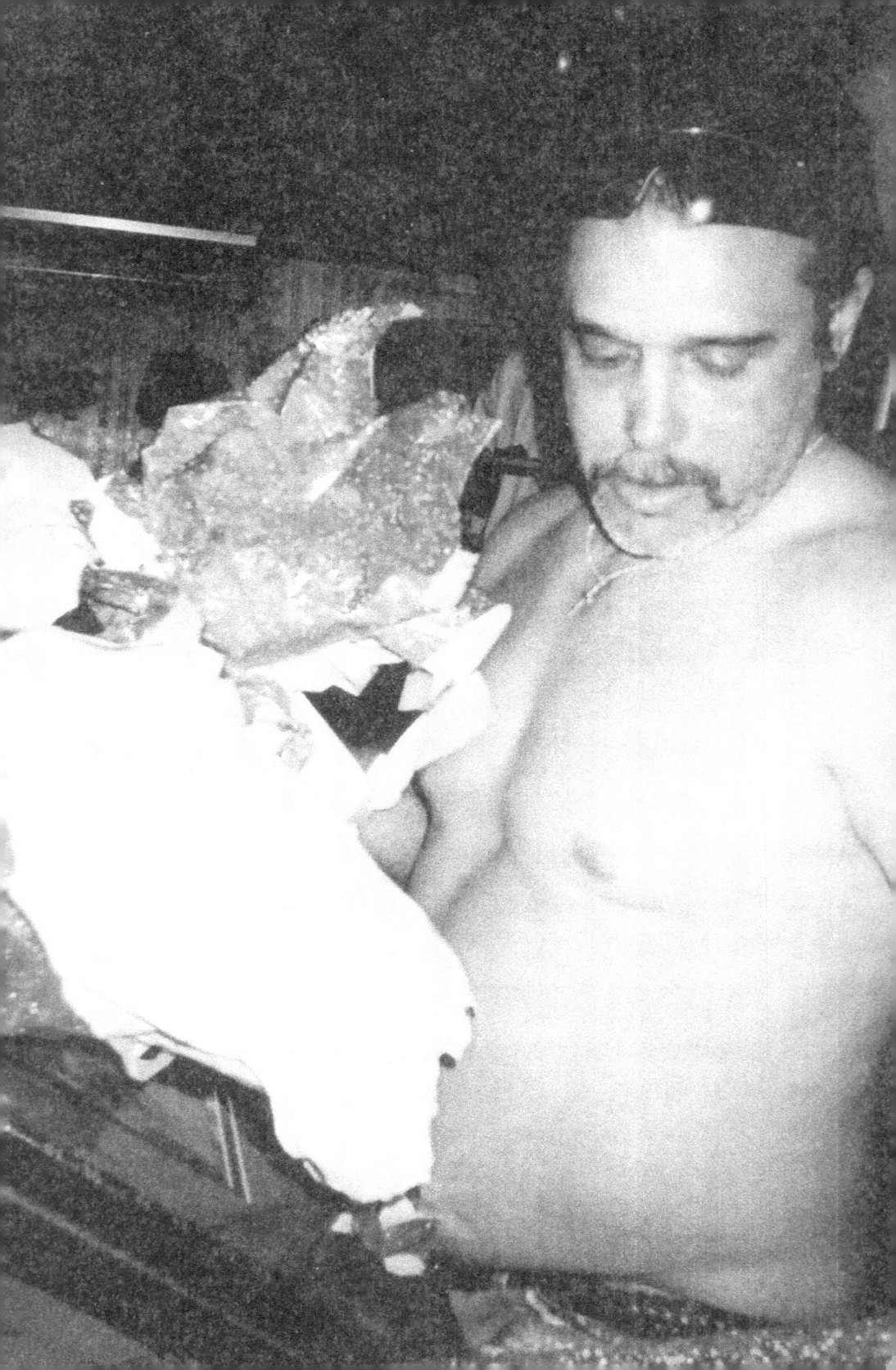

TO BATTLE THE BEAST

There is a man alive today who exists because mankind cannot survive alone;
Through history man has shown himself unable to battle the beast within his soul.
Man has come upon the point, in fact, from which no return can be perceived or known;
It is time that man sat down to evaluate anew those things which contradict His goal.

This man who lives is pure, and thereby left beyond the reach of all the sins of man;
His existence is such that He has no need to battle for what we call possessions.
His spirit is His mind, and He knows the end result of every useless mortal plan;
He is here today. He is ours and we are His, beyond the grasp of all obsessions.

THOMAS DANIEL TRIPLETT, SR.

CAN'T YOU SEE?

The forces of good are being defeated by the bonds they gather in good will;
Soon the bombs bursting will give us no thrill.
The rocket's red glare will be screaming our pride,
but toward targets where no living ears abide.
Can it never be that a man with the intelligence of Carl Sagan
can sit and talk of peace with men like Mr. Ronald Reagan?
Is it ironic that man's thus far triumphant quest of space
should also be the source and means by which we bring about
extinction of the human race?
People have become as animals and prey upon another's misfortunes;
It is embarrassing, the plots that man's conceived to bring about distortions.
I can look around and see the clouds expanding on every horizon in my sight;
I know that something isn't right.
O'ver the twilight's last gleaming I can see a dream that man will live;
O'er the ramparts I watch men die offering forth what they can give.
In the home of the brave a man must walk the streets and beg for food or steal;
On the land of the free there are many tombstones marking what is real.
A wino kneels in the alley-way and prays
while Congress votes itself another raise.
We are told our leaders strive to free us from our hate and greed,
but reality states another creed.
America.
In our country a junkie walks the streets and sells his mother for a dollar;

A policeman saves a cat and gets a medal for his valor.
Men are sent to jail for doing what they must to eat;
Our farmers are not growing wheat.
They've mortgaged their land to cover the cost of growing crops;
They cannot make a living selling produce in the shops.
I've been told since young of cutting off your nose to spite your face,
but I had not thought it was so commonplace.
A man must go in debt for twenty years to have a place in which he may reside;
He sells his bones to save his hide.
Our fathers brought forth unto this nation a dazzling array of prospects for the poor;
They did not see how the power of the rich would one day make us not so sure.
We are people and we do not have to have, like sheep, our actions guided;
We would like to have a say before the future is decided.
it is by democracy that we get a chance to air our view,
but in the politics involved we see a different hue;
In politics a man must do what it will take to gain a vote or make a buck;
and if by chance you interfere, you've used up all your luck.
To be or not to be is not to be at odds with what the law has deemed,
and give me liberty or give me death means nothing when the truth is gleaned.
Liberty is bought and sold like common shares of stock,
and justice is a system not so solid as a rock.
Who you are is by far more important than who you could ever hope to be;
Can't you see?

NOTHING

Nothing can exist without the time to be;
Nothing can be seen without an eye to see;
Nothing can exist without a place to live;
Nothing can be given without a means to give;
Nothing can be heard without an ear to hear;
Nothing can be close without it being near;
Nothing can be bought without it being sold;
Nothing can be ancient without it being old;
Nothing can be water without it being wet;
Nothing can be wagered without it being bet.

Somewhere there is truth and purity of mind;
Somewhere there is lost a sense I cannot find;
Somewhere there is love and trust to feel;
Somewhere there is what is real;
Somewhere there is life without a war;
Somewhere someone's senses aren't up to par;
Somewhere there is water running clean;
Somewhere there are trees that blossom green;
Somewhere there exists a touch of pleasure;
Somewhere there exists a place of treasure.

Nowhere is there justice in laws that we create;
Nowhere is there logic in theories we debate;
Nowhere is there practice in the honor that we preach;
Nowhere is there need to live within a niche;
Nowhere has our bombs instilled a trust;
Nowhere is there need to blast away earth's crust;
Nowhere is there sense in that we all must die;
Nowhere is there time which isn't passing by;
Nowhere is there joy in watching one another writhe;
Nowhere is there clean air we can breathe.

Somehow there's a way to find the goal;
Somehow there's a way to look into the soul;
Somehow there are mountains to be climbed;

Somehow there's a reason to be rhymed;
Somehow there's a need to see this through;
Somehow there's a need to say I grew;
Somehow numbers merge as one;
Somehow I will live to see the dawn;
Somehow day will pass into the night;
Somehow I will see the unseen sight.

Earth is where we find ourselves alive;
Earth is under roads on which we drive;
Earth is under water where we swim;
Earth is where our hope is getting slim;
Earth provides our fruits and meat;
Earth provides the ground to have a seat;
Earth is troubled and divided into nations;
Earth is where we struggle for relations;
Earth is people on their way through space;
Earth is home to the human race.

Time is an essence somewhat undermanned;
Time passes just the same in every land;
Time is felt, but no way can be seen;
Time is growth, but everything is lean;
Time is always here and never goes;
Time is passing now for foes;
Time is lost and man is at the wheel;
Time is now for saying what we feel;
Time is the end of all to come;
Time itself is losing some.

Love begins when pride and passion merge;
Love is made as heat and feelings surge;
Love is man's most awesome stream;
Love can make the strongest scream;
Love is the place to leave your problems bare;
Love is so much more than care;
Love is lust's most dearest aim;
Love is not some silly game;
Love is blowing in the breeze;
Love is yearned in great degrees.

THE DAY HAS RISEN

The day has risen on the eve of dawn,
upon the edge where time has gone.
There's no more life on earth to breathe,
so I call on Jesus for reprieve.

The edge of night is sizzled in the burn,
and there is nothing else to yearn.
With Jesus here to man the stern,
there is now so much to learn.

The rainbow didn't shine on our malfunctioned state,
as man heard not the calling from the Gate.
Man learned all to late
that there was no more time for hate.

Jesus gave His life to stop the sin,
all we had to do was let Him in.
Seek Christ's voice beyond the din,
and even now you can be men.

The air is thick with brimstone ash,
because some stupid men were rash.
All of earth is turned to trash
because of struggles over cash.

People we are running out of time;
Materials aren't worth a dime.
You've got to put an end to all this crime;
God gives something else to mime.

Let Jesus dwell inside your heart;
Learn His lesson, take a part.
There is no other way to start
to stop this tearing life apart.

PROSPEROUS INTENTIONS

What is this tendency I have to roam;
Why do I find myself so far from home?
In jail; this is no place for me;
It has no bearing on who I am to be.

My friends all east, no family have I here;
Nothing at all to hold too dear.
All I have are prosperous intentions,
but I got caught up in pretention.

I plan to lead the world one day,
to rid these humans their dismay.
The world is filled with evil men
fighting wars they cannot win.

Starvation and plagues and deaths of thirst;
Stop pronouncing which is worse.
You cannot make it all a game
when each one kills you just the same.

If love would be man's only task,
he'd find some sun in which to bask.
I know the things which should be banned:
The lies and hate and kicking sand.

In my struggles to exist upon the streets,
I saw the things that mankind greets:
Atheists, murderers, robbers and hookers have a ball;
I wonder if they think at all.

I've seen people launch some vicious ploy,
and act like life's a little toy.
What kind of life is that to live
when everyone takes but none will give?

This is not what God had on His mind
when He create what we find.
He gave us love to rule emotion,
and we have cast it to the ocean.

I find myself not far from home
no matter where I roam;
Each time I think that hope is gone,
God gives me strength to carry on.

MAN'S DEFICIENCY

Has the world not to offer me but pain and destitution?
If attacked, can I not demand some restitution?
If I seek naught but to battle man's deficiency
am I defeated through fear that I may learn efficiency?
I want nothing but for love to grown in all dimensions,
yet always hate surmounts the purest of intentions.
Groups are formed to ensure I be defeated,
and oft as not I find they have succeeded.
Evil mounts a force to wreak its devastation;
Ignoring all who seek its revocation.
Alone, I cannot halt this grand destruction;
I need somebody near to give instruction.
I am angered by the depravities called progression,
because they seem to me to be regression.
God spoke of this evil and its flourishment,
and how our crime keeps giving Satan nourishment.

MOTIONS OF LATITUDE

Fraudulent capacities overriding pure intention;
Corporate audacities usurping sure invention.
Radicalism multiplied, activating disconnection;
Cataclysms nullified, activating misconception.
People flagellated by motions of latitude;
Mentalities agitated by oceans of attitude.
Confusions dignified by man describing time;
Conclusions signified by man committing crime.
Wars decreed because man cannot take what's in his head;
Stars bereaved because our planet is near dead.
Treasures pragmatized by man's attempts to rule;
Pressures magnified by man's contempt of school.

THOMAS DANIEL TRIPLETT, SR.

WHEN NATIONS THRIVE AND PEOPLE COWER

It is a savage thing indeed which exists within my human mind;
A doubt that stands as real as any man may ever come to find.
From whence this doubt arrived I can name no time or place,
but I really feel sorry for the entire human race.

To me there is no bright avenues by which a man may grow and live;
Not even do most Christians feel the hope their words so often give.
In democracy the majority cannot ever win because the rich have all the power;
A world cannot live in peace when nations thrive and people cower.

In this all indeed there is a doubt for what the people may deserve;
God gave them Earth, but just as well an obligation to preserve.
Their greed for status in itself did crucify the only son that God would send,
and still He says that He is there if man should choose to make amend.

Man has grown, and now he has the power to destroy his earth in war;
Pieces of dust and debris could be what once was his home star.
Man pays no heed to the Karma involved in all that he may see and feel;
He doesn't seem to think that either God or psychic thought is real.

WHEN ALL IS SAID AND DONE

It's an achievement of man that science does seek the heights;
Today we stand in awe as our shuttles take their flights.
Men of breed play chess or football, whatever is their mind;
Our leaders fight with words or wars, however so inclined.

The people who are we must strive to live in peace,
while the people who are they seem to yearn to make us cease.
The consciousness of man will survive when all is said and done;
Bureaus count statistics that will last beyond the fun.

We vote for these people who but gladly take the helm,
and it seems that it is us they seek to overwhelm.
The audacity itself should be an end to all they seek to do,
but a populace confused will never see it through.

250 million people are doomed to die in the United States alone,
and overseas there is a chance that there won't even be a bone.
I can't begin to see how one would hate their brother so;
There earth is ours, but still we will not let our troubles go.

Tell me how it is that we must die as soldiers fighting war
when we were placed as brethren on this star.
The people on this globe do not deserve this kind of death,
but the meager man is slow to raise his breath.

THOMAS DANIEL TRIPLETT, SR.

WHAT WILL YOU HAVE LEFT TO SAY?

I look to the horizon, yet cannot see;
I am no slave, yet, I am not free.
My heart is depressed, I want to fight;
I must defend what I think is right.

Time just races by, it's never slow;
We gain our knowledge and still don't know.
We cherish our lives and hold them dear,
never understanding quite why we're here.

We look at each other and try to be serious,
but a look at the world shows we're delirious.
All the blame is placed upon the youth,
and they revolt because they know the truth.

Our technology has soared the heights,
but we only talk of human rights.
We've traveled far since our distant past,
but how much longer can we last?

With buttons pushed and life destroyed,
when earth becomes a lifeless void,
what will you have left to say?
Would you have said it yesterday?

People say I'm dumb to say these things,
but I can't help it if some truth stings.
We've lost our cheer by seeking joy;
We've only morals that destroy,

You could say you didn't realize,
that truth had such a good disguise,
but you'll lie and say you knew no facts
even though you heard of all the pacts.

You can never falsify the truth,
nor seek to disavow the proof;
You've split our thoughts with little lies,
and pushed the end into our lives.

WHERE ARE RIGHTS?

Where are rights for men who seek to live a life aside from harm?
Can he gain no separation from this ever-growing human swarm?
A man, himself, should be allowed to choose his fate,
never mind diplomacy or what you think is waiting at the Gate.

Laws were never meant to subjugate a man throughout his life;
Economy wasn't designed that man should spend his time in strife.
I yearn so much to have this burden lifted from my mind;
There is so much more on earth that I could find.

I once was forced to spend a stretch of time in jail,
and I gained a sense for how the atmosphere of life goes stale;
An awareness of things that forever seem to strain and haunt me,
and an ability to look beyond this mess and see.

Such joy that peace is breaking out across our planet earth;
Too bad that man has yet to recognize its worth.
What is freedom in a life that takes away your breath?
Where are rights for men who seek to live aside from death?

OMIT THE LIQUID

I will venture now to step beyond the brink;
Omit the liquid please, I've had enough to drink.
Though if it's Scotch I could stand a little more;
It doesn't matter, I've finished keeping score.

With my mind aloft these clouds are pretty dense;
Millions of people here, but none are making any sense.
It seems they've all derived a different plan
for making man a caring clan.

Each one quite intent that theirs should be the one;
They'll sacrifice the next as if he were a pawn.
They've no concern that I've a better notion;
They'll kill me too if I stir up commotion.

I've often wondered how this nonsense can appear;
How it's conquered all the thing we hold so dear.
They're fighting wars to precipitate a time of peace;
Pleading love, and yet their hatred will not cease.

THOMAS DANIEL TRIPLETT, SR.

I CANNOT TELL

As I look around I cannot doubt that I am here;
But for a call, I wouldn't have a reason.
I strain my eyes so as to see both far and near,
but I sense no time of day or season.

A stranger cast upon a land I do not know
to survive by methods all so odd to me;
I feel as though alone no matter where I go,
as though imprisoned in a place I should not be.

The water, land and people all around me are so kind,
yet there exists a savagery for which I have no need;
It is as though I was in some way left behind
to observe this human breed.

I see and hear it all but do not seem to be a part.
I cannot be assured by the records of my birth,
because I was not allowed to make the chart
and therefore cannot judge their worth.

This planet is much indeed too small for me,
but I can't tell from where I came.
Perhaps there is a God who made me be,
but I don't know his name.

I wish so much to go where I belong,
to travel on until I find my home.
It seems an inner voice keeps urging me along,
and it will not let me cease to roam.

It says I'm here, but that I cannot stay;
It says to travel far and wide but never rest.
It says to go, and I feel I must obey;
It says that I must pass the test.

I observe these humans and discern a wild creature.
Civilization? I know not where they heard the name.
Each one thinks he is the feature,
the reason for the game.

But there are no features and this is no game.
Still I must travel, observe and learn;
to seek ways in which these humans can be tame,
to prevent a war in which their earth will burn.

Humans burden me with their senseless acts;
Slaying my heart and tearing down my mind
with their inability to see the facts,
and their disregard for anything of the kind.

A LESSON OF DUPLICITY

I observed a rainbow and its purpose slowly came to view;
A relevance activated on the conscious of quite few.
I witnessed as a squirrel hoarded nuts for hibernation,
and I became assured that man was born through hybridization.

I pondered the eagle and its advantage far beyond its prey,
and there came to me a vision of startling array;
A detonated bomb, and mankind scurries in regress,
no longer to avoid philosophies they thought they could suppress.

I watched a beaver falling trees in preparation for his dam,
and queried quite at depth the thoughts of men like Uncle Sam.
Indeed we thought him just, for he's the man our voting crowned,
but his ways may cause this country's razing to the ground.

I watched a lizard darting from the crevice serving as his home,
and became quite awed at seas that bubble boiled bone.
I saw this all in the briefest moment you can contemplate,
and I was at a loss for what there is to compensate.

I knew right then that there was no way I could take a stand;
Matters have progressed too vastly out of hand.
I thought perhaps that now would be the time to try,
but the sun was too distinctly hidden in the sky.

Where are our minds of old; Aristotle, Plato and Demosthenes,
Is all their wisdom given off to have atrocities?
I've asked around, and there's none who can soothe my fears;
The thoughts I mention only flood their eyes with tears.

The uses of our technologies have arrived upon decrepitude,
and our philosophies are carried on by people of ineptitude.
We've allowed primordial capacities to invade our intelligence,
and we will surely lose those things we call embellishments.

Philosophy combines stability, proficiency and wisdom in civility;
Technology has given us the means to have senility.
Its loss would not upset our foreign policies,
but only bring an end to silly fallacies.

THOMAS DANIEL TRIPLETT, SR.

PERCEPTION

What keener perception I have of things,
seeing them much clearer than before.
My life has ventured where it sings,
sensing pleasure to the core.

I've attained a sharper attitude
about the things I know;
I can't say it's latitude,
but I've got lines to show.

I can plan out life much better now
because of portions I can see,
but I don't remember when or how
these parts became so clear to me.

I can but wonder how I found the way,
when things are surely now as they were then,
but somehow now I think it's safe to say
that I think I'm gonna win.

These thoughts came lunging up at me,
coming from I can't say where;
Somehow demanding that they be,
they've given cause to really care.

In a flash I caught my drift,
the same old vison with a different hue;
Colors too intense to sift,
wisdom seeping through.

These things I've thought of in the past,
but now they're altered some, I'm sure;
So many characters in a cast,
so few roles that may endure.

These thoughts are here before they leave,
giving the advantage that they can.
The past is something I perceive,
but now to walk where once I ran.

It's like I died, and now I live;
A thing that happened once before.
I see now what I have to give,
and what I can restore.

It matters naught when things go wrong,
as actions always pave the way.
I can't sit back, and won't wait long;
I've got some things that I must say.

A life once well involved with thugs,
I had no care for hope,
but since I've cut out all the drugs
I've found a way to cope.

My life is as a shining star,
and I the keeper of its light;
I can see things near or far,
and know things hidden from my sight.

I need some time to fit the parts,
to build a base that's steady,
But if I avoid the phony starts
I'm sure I now am ready.

I see a whole new start for me,
safer than the one I saw.
Security is the thing I see
if I obey the law.

All these things seem very new,
but it's the way I've always thought;
Maybe in this change of view
a saner way is sought.

Enough of standing in the dark
when I've a dream worth catching.
I am going to make my mark,
or at least an etching.

In stepping out I find I'm clean
I can disregard the things I've done.
God knows well that which I mean,
so I can have some fun.

I owe myself the things I missed,
and perhaps I'll have a chance to get them back.
I didn't make some silly list,
but I think I am on track.

I don't know this change that's taken place,
and it doesn't matter if I do,
if I can show it in my face
perhaps it'll start in you.

It makes me happy to see myself as good,
to know that I've found the way;
I'm feeling like I always should,
and happy every day.

DARKNESS CLOSING IN

The wisdom gathered in his years;
A rickety old man, feeble in his age.
His eyes are dry, he sheds no tears;
Unable to shake his finger in a rage.

Who is he now, what about his past,
or his friends of days gone by?
Dead; He is the last,
this old decrepit guy.

Lost in a world which no longer cares,
he stands there with his back against the wall.
People passing unawares;
The buildings are so tall.

The skies, it seems, have lost their blue,
and the streets aren't made of dirt.
Airplanes roar where eagles flew;
it's so hard to stay alert…

With this darkness closing in
he hasn't the vision he had before.
He must die to live again;
Pieces leaving more and more…

With these shaky knees he cannot stand,
so he collapses to the walk.
None passing by will lend a hand,
nor even stop to talk.

He pulls his knees up to his chest;
Why is passing always cold?
He lived his life just like the rest,
and one day he got old…

Darkness now, nothing but the moon,
and there is someone nudging at his arm.
In his mind there plays a tune
from a time when he was young and warm.

Glancing up, a smile on his face,
he sees a man in blue.
He laughs, he cries, there's no disgrace;
He simply states his time is through…

This cannot happen, says the cop,
B=but his words have fallen through the air;
We go on living until we stop,
and now and then we care…

Right there, the phone; have you got a dime?
The rush, all chaos; something must be done.
Dying here is not a crime,
but what about our fun?

So many sirens screaming down the street;
Is everyone messed up in the head?
His passing on was so discreet,
but all the same he's dead.

People gather close to see this face of death,
as if their being here now could give him aid,
But when he took his final breath
none had attention to be paid…

On the stretcher now, beneath a sheet;
Clean him up to put him in a grave.
Hand a name tag from his feet,
and remember he was brave…

IT CAUSES ME REGRESS

I awoke this morning to the humming of a Rush,
and it bent my mind like a strawberry slush;
I thought of life and the ideal dream,
and considered having coffee without the cream.

I thought of love, and the chances I've discarded;
My alarm went off, and the day got started.
It happens in life that I'm a sucker for distress,
though oft as not it causes me regress.

I pulled the curtains back, and opened my front door;
I really didn't want to open up the store.
Scrambled eggs and biscuits were heavy on my mind,
as well as other things that cannot be defined.

I can't ignore the dampness of the early morning rain,
but there is something else to occupy my brain;
Upon inspecting life I've found an empty space:
I need a woman bad, and nothing else will take her place.

I yearn for the past, knowing I can't have it back;
Some things occur from which you get no slack.
I've lost my family somehow as I've grown;
Some things occur for which a reason isn't known.

I simply haven't got, I guess, what it takes to keep in touch;
Sometimes the trouble is too much.
I need to have a lady by my side;
The road through life is mighty wide.

Without attention, a woman tends to slip away;
She needs devotion every single day.
It's plain and simple reality, you must pay the price;
But sometimes it gets lonely being nice.

WILL YOU LISTEN?

How can I listen to people wo don't inspire trust?
Why should I dig beneath the crust?
I cannot understand people who are always on the guard;
What in life could be so hard?

If I tell you something that I did,
it's so that nothing will be hid,
so don't try taking what I say
and twisting it some other way.

People in high positions make me mad
when they treat me as if I'm bad;
Their contradictions put my mind in great disdain,
because they started somewhere, true and plain.

I simply can't accept their every word
knowing of the treachery that I've heard.
Instead of bearing down on folks like me,
why don't they open their eyes and see?

They created the life that people cannot care about,
and omitted the things that may well help us out.
I cannot work in what I think to be a useless field;
I am proud, and I won't yield.

If I don't pay attention to the laws they speak,
it's because I know their plan is weak.
I know the havoc they have wrought,
and I know they are distraught.

I rarely mess with powerful emotions,
and I seldom follow funny notions,
but I know they want me to live
by whatever conditions they may give.

They provide no proper way to be,
and condemn my thoughts when I don't see;
The earth itself is very old,
but history can't be sold.

The truth is there for us to find;
We already know it in our mind.
It's been right there for us to see,
both you and me.

Scientists shouldn't take the blame
for all the politician's shame;
Our leaders are the ones who make us lose,
and we can't even choose.

TIME PASSES BY

Let it be thus spoken:
Our life is just a token,
nothing but a fallacy
arranged around a policy.
You live, you die;
Time passes by.

All you do is play your games;
Other people, other names.
Scenes are changed for different view;
Nothing changes but the hue.
You live, you die;
Time passes by.

Dream your dreams and hope your hopes,
someone else still holds the ropes.
You can buck and fight to have your way,
but you simply have no say.
You live, you die;
Time passes by.

You gather fortunes learning how to live,
but what have you to give?
Some time, perhaps, for a friend in need,
or are you lost in greed?
You live, you die;
Time passes by.

SOUTH JAKEGEAR

Many years ago
a man set out with wishes;
He dreamed that he'd find gold,
but all he found were dishes.

One day he was growing tired,
and lost all hope and wishes,
news came that an old friend was fired;
Jake felt sad and sent the man some dishes.

Now come to pass,
a miner came to him;
At long and finally last
his future wasn't dim.

This miner brought him news,
and it was said
that Jake jumped out of his shoes.
Amazing, for he was almost dead.

The news was of a kid,
a part-time banana peeler.
He got for those dishes a very high bid
from an antique dealer.

So if you ever find yourself in South Jakegear
and hear of people who crazily ran,
you've no cause for fear.
It's caused by the ghost of that happy old man.

TO MAKE OF THINGS

Where has the joy of unity gone
Is there plurality in what we've won?
We have existed since the dawn,
but can we truly carry on?

We have squabbles and murder every day;
It seems corruption is the way.
If our politicians have their say
I think we'll be blown away.

We have lost the morals of our birth
by living life for all it's worth?
All around we wade in mirth;
What has happened to our earth?

We have heard of Socrates and Seth;
We know of Hitler and Macbeth.
The one will seek to give us breath,
the other only urges death.

I think of all the goals we've sought,
and all the pleasures we were taught.
That is where we all get caught;
From whence the havoc we have wrought.

We sought to somehow change the scheme,
to somehow rearrange the theme.
But God and nature are a team,
to make of things as They may deem.

Bombs are made to kill our brother,
and plots are made to wreck each other.
Pollution in the air, we smother;
On the brink, and yet we hover.

BLUE MOMENTS

They come upon us every now and then,
if only to remind us that we are men;
The thoughts of how good life may have been
always let them in.

You know who you are and what you could be,
but you must take a path by which you can't see.
In these blue moments you know you're not free,
because there isn't a place to which you can flee.

The victory is yours in this life you lead,
yet somehow it's lost in the throws of greed.
You know you can manage your every need,
yet from somewhere there comes an evil seed.

You're a champion, if only you're left alone;
You find the solutions that must be known.
You'll uncover the past that must be shown,
if someone has the time to loan.

It was but a while ago that you got your birth;
Now you so proudly roam the earth.
You think your life may have some worth,
but you must get beyond the mirth.

Your younger days are all now gone;
Even to the present you can't hold on.
All you can do is remember the battles you've won,
and hope your heart and mind are one.

The years, the months, the weeks and days;
Not a moment ever stays.
If you could only somehow catch the strays,
you could avoid the bluest ways.

BECAUSE OF ROLES ASSUMED

I'm so tired of meeting people who pretend,
themselves unsure of where they stand.
Living as though the play will never end,
they're building castles with watered sand.

Built on an image that isn't really there,
the likeness also fades before the sun.
They merely shift into another scene
to form an impression for another cast.

Identities lost because of roles assumed,
these people live forever in a void.
What is love when treated as mirage?
Will it not dissolve when reality approaches?

I'm tired of the very action of entrapment,
of people who exist in any way you them to.
Having no substance that they can call their own,
they come and go like phantoms in the night.

Do you, too, exist because of what I may perceive,
or are you really there?
Are you a dream inspired by a dream,
or were you here before?

SENSING COMFORT

I have a compass here, but still I feel ill at ease;
Where am I, would someone tell me please?
I heard an organ grinding in my ear,
and then some movement brought me here.

I have a compass, but I can get no bearing.
Perfect vision, but only darkness where I'm staring.
I have balance, but what is up or down?
From whence this chill I feel all around?

I breathe, but I know my air is going fast;
These moments well could be my last.
The ecstasy to think I've found the tomb;
The collapse that well could mean my doom.

Alas, my lungs have ceased to be efficient;
The air in my cells won't be sufficient.
My colleagues knew I thought this was the sight;
They thought me crazy, but I was right.

My shell is dead, for God now beckons me;
The earth is gone, and I must make my plea.
A plea for the pleasure I awaited;
An assurance that all my pain has been abated.

ANGER

Have you really ever thought
about what anger is?
It's really quite hard to define
yet it lurks in every mind.
Like a bird in a cage,
it yearns to be set free.

Some people keep it under love and dreams,
but for others that's impossible.
So if you're feeling down and out,
keep this thought in mind:
Everyone has times when they get mad;
The only difference in a soul
is if you feel bad when you lose control.

IF EVERYONE WOULD STOP

If everyone would stop and look around at things,
they'd see they've caused a flop with all their flings.
If everyone would stop and look at what they've done,
they'd see that their own actions have them on the run.

If everyone would stop and think of what to do,
they'd surely find an answer fit and true.
Just believe in themselves and put forth what they've got,
and know that love will stop the rot.

THOMAS DANIEL TRIPLETT, SR.

113

A LONELY PLACE

Death doesn't scare me;
It's coming, I can see.
No matter what I have to say
I cannot make it turn away.

I won't be dumb
and wait for it to come,
as there are better things to do
before this life is through.

Death hasn't any season,
and often strikes without a reason.
Nobody gets to air their voice,
as death does make the final choice.

Death is very cozy
to anyone who gets too nosy.
Coffins are made for those who sleep,
and those who live can only weep.

It doesn't choose between young and old,
it merely makes your body cold.
Cemetery populations grow,
as you well know.

A grave is such a lonely place,
feeding off the human race.
Millions of tombstones well inscribed,
but death has never been described.

TWISTED

What are these thoughts my mind has wrung?
What are these words which miss my tongue?
I know the thoughts, and what they're all about,
but I just can't seem to spit them out.

I still recall your warmth right there beside me,
and I wonder how this parting came to be.
I only wanted to give my love to,
but you've decided you have something else to do.

I asked you frankly if there was a cause to name,
and you tell me there is neither fault nor blame.
In the beginning I know your love was mine,
but you took it back at the finish line.

There was so much I thought I had to give,
and now you tell me that I cannot live.
Why must it be the case that I am out the door?
Why can't I just know the score?

I love you girl, this does pain me so;
I can't understand this letting go.
I've yearned too long for you to be my wife
to see any reason for this strife.

You've caused this ache inside my brain,
and I don't think I can take the pain.
My heart feels pierced as with a blade,
and the fluid inside cannot be staid.

I can accept the fact that there is nothing I can do;
There is nothing that you said which I may misconstrue.
I must look inside and find a way to let you go,
No matter what I know.

HAVE A REASON

Relay to me the feelings deep within your heart;
Tell me what they are and let me be a part.
You've no need to live life in dejection,
let me give you harbor from rejection.

If you get dizzy, don't try living life in grief,
Let me make your troubles brief.
You've no need to struggle for your air,
let me offer you a chair.

Relax, and let me share your time of ease;
I'm begging baby, please.
Explore your mind for the answers that resist;
You must have a reason to exist.

There are people who would try to bring you down,
and some of them would let you drown;
Let me offer you some precious days
to live apart from all the haze.

You need to stop and let your troubles pass you by,
take rest beneath a lazy summer sky.
You must have beginnings for any trip you take,
let me show you what a difference I can make.

Never float upon a sea that offers you no port,
and don't attempt to sell your glory short.
Separate yourself from all this social grime
and let me love you up until the end of time.

NO HARM

How came such a one as you to be?
From whence this person that I see?
Enigmas always seem to challenge me,
and I must say you've set one free.

A being synonymous with haze,
evasive essence in a maze,
not a master it obeys,
a cast of characters it portrays.

A shadow never really seen,
a forest fully paved in green,
a bay of torrent now serene,
a land where all is shiny clean.

Questions posed on purpose just to scout,
as below the surface swims a trout;
in your head there lives a doubt,
but you're not sure what it's about.

At once attracted by your charm,
I've found that you are really warm.
Assured that you will bring no harm,
I've got you have you in my arms.

I CAME TO THE BELIEF

Though I never made the inquisition
when we first met I seemed to be an imposition.
I was in such a terrible disposition
that I didn't think to ask permission.

In providing a house in which I could recline
you gave me an offer I couldn't decline.
For what developed I was not inclined;
Indeed the thought had never crossed my mind.

I had tired of life and sought release,
and I knew we could live in peace.
Then the feelings started to increase,
and it was clear they wouldn't cease.

You were all so worried you'd be burned
that you wouldn't acknowledge what you yearned,
But it wasn't long until you learned
that your emotions can't be spurned.

I'm glad you took the time to make correction,
because I really couldn't take rejection.
You came to me as with infection,
and I was your injection.

Now it seems I'm used up like a chair,
and it simply isn't fair.
If you don't love me any more, just say the word;
it will be heard.

But if you love me, I insist you let me know;
I can't be just your bro.
I must decide which way to go;
It's either yes or no.

WITH RAIN UPON THE AIR

Once before, with rain upon the air,
I pondered just how much I really care.
I thought, back then, that it would make no sense
for me to try to climb your fence.

But now I've had you in my arms,
and felt the comfort of your charms.
I have shared the pleasure in your smile,
and I've found I need it all the while.

I thought, back then, that you were not for me,
but I wasn't sure how that could be.
Once before, with rain upon the air,
I pondered just much I really care.

But now I have said hello to you,
and none else will ever do.
I find that I have given you my heart
in every tiny little part.

I have touched the way you work your mind,
and I'm entranced by what I find.
I know that we have got the tools
to make our love start forming pools.

WHY THE SNEER?

In many positions of thought have I been placed,
and through times undated have I raced.
Thoughts flow through my head that will not cease,
consistent in the main of freedom, love and peace.

Looking at something as vast as our sky,
I know mine is but to live and die.
But if I try, what goals will I seek?
Will the adventure make my spirit weak?

I ask questions to find the answers I must know.
Some sound strange, but what's to show?
With no answers for the questions I may ask,
how may I fulfill my task?

Love means more to me than anything else,
For happiness consists of nothing else.
It fills one's head with many funny notions;
It is the strongest of emotions.

Do I do what I want because it's the way I feel,
or do I avoid that which is real?
If it's done because of what I feel, then why the sneer?
Is it more important just to please a peer?

SADNESS REACHES OUT FROM ME

You say that I really disappointed you,
but you won't listen to my words.
You've been enraged over something I didn't do,
and the whole thing's really quite absurd.

I now proclaim that it was you who did the wrong
by ignoring what I had to say.
You said your love for me was strong,
but it didn't take too much to sway.

The kind of love I had to give
was love beyond a lie,
the kind of love to live
until I die.

I truly wanted you to wed
into my life,
but you have chosen much instead
to bring me only strife.

And now the thing I never had in mind to do
will surly come to be;
I must spend my life away from you,
adrift in open sea.

I will know I love you, but it will never come to good.
I must deal with the things I see
since you told me where I stood.
What ever else could be?

I pray I never see you anymore
for the time you've put me through,
because I see fit to justify the score
and that would never do.

I could sum it up to say I love you,
if you'd just get off my brain.
What would I do
if I saw you standing in the rain?

THOMAS DANIEL TRIPLETT, SR.

NOT A PAWN

I hope you know that I can never be a slave,
as slaves have none of love to give.
You seem to have a charm I crave,
but I must breathe if I'm to live.

Don't seek to have me follow every whim
as a test to see how much I care;
My thoughts are governed by a gem,
but I must see the light somewhere.

Don't ever try to gain the upper hand
as a way to see who has more strength;
My life is not so hard to understand
if you view it in its length.

Never try to solely rule my heart
from fear that I may soon be gone.
Realize in every part
that I am not a pawn.

SUCH A THING TO SEE

How can I describe the way I feel
when beauty stands before me?
I'm amazed there's such a thing to see,
astonished that it's real.

I cannot wait to get her off alone,
to see what's on her mind.
What is there for me to find?
Are there things unknown?

I see them come, I see them go;
None is to acquire.
But of each I must inquire
if she has love to know.

I would take her anyplace,
and treat her as I must,
but first I must find trust,
and there's little in the human race.

She may never know how much I care,
but she would always have my heart.
There is not a better way to start
than with a woman fair.

I'd like to hear the things she has to say,
because I'd like to please her so,
but I'd quickly let her go
if she had some game to play.

With all the lies alive on earth,
truth I simply must demand;
I find it awful hard to understand
what anything else is worth.

Some people have a beauty to be seen
and others have it in their heart,
but now and then there is a part
that meets them in between.

Some have beauty shining through their eyes
and other have it in their soul,
but there are some who have it as a whole
and offer you no alibis.

I love the thought of growing grey
and feeling like a little boy.
I want to have my piece of joy,
there's nothing more to say.

SOMETIMES I LOOK AROUND

Sometimes I look around and I cannot see my dream;
My thoughts are like a wild, foaming stream.
Sometimes I look around and nothing seems quite right;
My hopes, my wishes fading out of sight.

Sometimes I look around and see sorrow in a crowd;
I know it hurts when men are proud.
Sometimes I look around and see sorrow etched upon a face;
I know it hurts when a man can't find his place.

Sometimes I look around and the walls are painted gray;
I know first hand the pain of having gone astray.
Sometimes I look around and a frown awaits a smile;
I know that things are getting harder all the while.

Sometimes I look around and see people looking back at me;
I know that people yearn to set their burden free.
Sometimes I look around at the flowers in the field,
and I know our fate is sealed.

Sometimes I look around at a sky crammed full of stars,
and I know that man is plagued with wars.
Sometimes I look around and think of love and hate,
and I wonder what it was that caused the great debate.

Sometimes I look around and we are cattle grazing out a swath;
I've never had a problem understanding math.
Sometimes I look around as tourists stop to see the view,
and I wonder if they see it in another hue.

Sometimes I look around seeking comfort from my grief,
but when it comes it's always very brief.
Sometimes I look around to see if I can find a reason,
and indeed I know the chill that's in the season.

Sometimes I look around and I know you really care,
because I've never known another quite so fair.
Sometimes I look around and see the breezes blow;
I sense your smile keeping me aglow.

THOMAS DANIEL TRIPLETT, SR.

A COMFORT

I can travel through the land of misty dreams,
or through the forest of shadow thought,
because nothing is ever as it seems;
Leaving, always losing what I sought.

Finding patterns where flower blossoms grew,
or orchards where deserts once would scorch,
but does it matter if it's true?
Leaving, darkness where once there flamed a torch.

Arriving in a world void of light,
or in a time where reason has not been,
nothing ever seems quite right;
Leaving, never finding honest men.

Feeling the necessity of return to earth,
it feels good to have you standing there.
Few people since my time of birth
have seemed to really care.

In the morning I see the sun, so warm;
it gives me what I need to start.
But later, when I have you in my arms,
is when I feel the stirring in my heart.

A comfort that arrived, I guess, with years;
Perhaps, in part, because I know I am your guy.
I want to lift your hopes, erase your fears,
make you laugh when you would really rather cry.

I would tell you things none else may know,
and listen to what no other person would.
I would have you with me no matter where I go,
and explain some things you never fully understood.

Just love me and let me know that you are there.
Make me aware of what you really feel,
and I will always show you just how much I care.
I will never do a thing I must conceal.

THOMAS DANIEL TRIPLETT, SR.

NO PLACE, NO TIME, NO WAY

No place to turn, no place to cry,
no place to hide, no time for tears to dry,
no time for apologies, they come too late;
Only remorse in my sad state.

No place for love, no place for dreams;
Nothing is ever as happy as it seems.
No time to say that I was wrong,
Just gone, as though I don't belong.

No place that I can live,
nothing I can give,
no time for going back to change your mind;
No way to change today, no matter what I find.

Only mistakes and sorrow in my sight;
no time right now to soar the heights,
no time to stop and mend my heart,
only to hope it doesn't fall apart.

And fall apart it will, if I must think of you,
so I must think of something else to do.
If I cannot have you for a wife
I must erase you from my life.

BEYOND TODAY

I have all too often been with dames
who have a need to play their games.
They speak of love and how they really care,
but then their head is full of air.

I just notice all the words that fly
when they try making me their guy.
About the time I think I have a jewel,
it appears I was a fool.

All the words we whispered in our heat
mean nothing standing on our feet.
They plot and scheme to have their selfish way,
never caring much beyond today.

Diamonds strewn all through their home
is all that matters in their bones.
They have no ability to open up their mind,
and no desire for anything of the kind.

I want a love that I am sure I feel,
I cannot wonder if the words are real.
I want a mind that I can meet,
a heart to hold, a soul to greet.

THOMAS DANIEL TRIPLETT, SR.

IN THE LAND

In the land of the twilight moon,
with the sun to arrive quite soon,
I pump hot air to my balloon
to soar above the desert dune.

In the land alive with scorching heat,
with bubbles appearing on my feet,
I seek some place to take a seat
and think about my naval fleet.

In the land above the greenest earth,
with flowers blossomed to their worth,
I arrived one day in human birth,
to grow and build my hearth.

In the land of the constant feast,
where hunger has quite surely ceased,
I seek to make each man a piece;
There is for life another lease.

In the land where dreams can quickly turn to fact,
with peace and love not ever lacked,
I seek in honesty to make a pact,
to ensure that man will have his tract.

In the land where war would never dare appear,
where citizens hold their peace so very dear,
I would find it dreary without you near,
because my thoughts would not be clear.

IT IS RAINING NOW

It is raining now,
and I have nothing pressing I must do.
I cleared my mind of petty thoughts,
and all I left was you.
Millions of raindrops
falling in an awesome stream,
Force is measured sure
when a gale wind can scream.

It is cold indeed,
but your warmth is on my mind,
and I need nothing else to find.
I hear a truck
loading up to leave the scene;
Then I wondered what was true,
what it was I'd felt and seen.

I wonder what it was you felt
the night you shared yourself with me,
and I wonder if you gave a thought
to what could come to be.
I wondered then,
but I had no means to grant the motion,
so I passed it off
as another case of wishful notion.

You offered my mind an easy moment
for a breath of air,
and I will not forget
the passion we did share.
It's hard to write without an insight
as to what you have to say,
but pardon me if I attempt it anyway.

It is raining now,
so my mind may take a dozen turns;
Maybe I will stop to give a thought
to what each person yearns:
We yearn the coming of a day
of peace and freedom realized,
and we yearn to have love conquer
everything beneath the skies.

When will people realize
that they are sharing dreams of hope,
the multiples who believe
that love will always cope?
Tons of water raining down
upon my roof;
There are demons here among us
who would hide the truth.

You asked me if I'd changed,
and I think it might be so,
but who knows how these things may go?
Being in jail taught me respect
for what it takes to keep in line,
and I learned that often I must fight
for keeping what is mine.

I've shed the shyness that I had
because I had to shout for what I needed.
I learned the virtue given patience
because warnings often went unheeded.
Today I speak outright,
because I want to show intentions;
I learned that thoughts and words
are more than mere conventions.

They may seem insane at times,
but they are meant to aid;
Help is but a piece of jade.
By staying inside
I can keep from getting wet,
but I've often found the warmth to dry
in the people that I've met.

It is raining now,
and I have nothing else to say.
It's gotten pretty late,
near time to hit the hay.
Millions of raindrops
falling in an awesome stream.
Force is measured sure
when a gale wind can scream.

THOMAS DANIEL TRIPLETT, SR.

MAKE PLAIN
THE ENDING

Follow the trail your labor chops,
and make plain the ending where it stops.
Implant an image of your need;
Dispel delusions and their greed.

If you should hope to plot your course,
you've age-old wisdom for a source.
Given sense beyond the sanest beast,
you shall be the victor at the feast.

WITHOUT YOU I'D BE LOST

I am here to keep you in good cheer,
and cast aside your fear,
so if you're troubled or feeling low,
come to me so I may know.

I am concerned for how you feel;
My love for you is real!
Your eyes portray a picture of the sun,
and in your arms my chores are done.

You chase away the gloom of rain
to be the heat that cures my pain.
To have you near is to be tall;
Let me catch you when you fall.

If I've done something and you're mad,
come to me before it's bad;
I will always try for you,
but you must tell me how I do.

I'll not obey your every word
as such a thing is quite absurd,
but I'll make you happy, spare no cost;
Without you I'd be lost.

Whatever is mine is also yours,
never mind with keeping scores.
Just follow me closely and keep at hand,
And wear my wedding band.

A million things I want to do,
but they are all quite few;
All you have to do is ask,
and you will be my only task.

Nothing is too hard for me,
expect perhaps to drain the sea.
I'll live my life without a frown
if you put on a wedding gown.

I am here to keep you in good cheer,
and cast aside your fear;
I'll make you happy, spare no cost,
because without you I'd be lost.

THOMAS DANIEL TRIPLETT, SR.

❀ My Dear Daughter ❀

"If ever there is tomorrow
when we're not together...
there is something you must always
remember. You are braver than you
believe, stronger than you seem,
and smarter than you think.
But the most important thing is,
even if we're apart...
I'LL ALWAYS BE WITH YOU."

Felicity Triplett was 😢 feeling sad.
December 30, 2014 · 🌎

I really miss my dad but I know he isn't suffering no more now that he is in heaven with Jesus and I know he loved me he passed yesterday at 2:15 p.m. and I miss him so much!!!!!

Hope Triplett I love you baby girl. Here for you always.
December 30, 2014 at 7:39pm · Like

Felicity Triplett I no i love you
December 30, 2014 at 7:39pm · Like

Jason P Golden I love you all
December 30, 2014 at 8:28pm · Like

Tamara N Matthew Murdock love u felicity if u need anything im here...
December 30, 2014 at 8:49pm · Like

Cherish Daniels Love u felicity
December 30, 2014 at 9:15pm · Like

Tracy Triplett I love u. I may not be near but I am there for you and ur brothers if u need me.
December 30, 2014 at 9:57pm · Like

Falesha Lynn Carr I love you Felicity Triplett even if I am miles away
December 31, 2014 at 6:57am · Like

Mabel Brown so sorry
December 31, 2014 at 8:42am · Like

Kandice Golden I love you
December 31, 2014 at 9:38am · Like

Makyla Sheila Jacintho My prayers are with your family... so sorry to hear about Tom
December 31, 2014 at 10:56am · Like

Pam Ballett Triplett Love you
December 31, 2014 at 1:32pm · Like

Trinity Bell Sorry about your loss
December 31, 2014 at 9:33pm · Like 👍 1

Arianna Hudson sorry hope you feel better

December 31, 2014 at 9:52pm · Edited · Like

Misty Knorr Im so sorry Felicity Triplett i hope you are doing ok if ya need anything let me know. Your dad loved you to the moon amd back and he may not be here but you know he is always with you in your heart and watches over you everyday sis love u guys
December 31, 2014 at 9:53pm · Like

Angela Pruitt Voyles I am so sorry I didn't know your dad passed away
February 15, 2015 at 2:37pm · Like

Angela Pruitt Voyles Amanda Triplett sorry
February 15, 2015 at 2:38pm · Like

Note from the Publisher

Are you a first time author?

Not sure how to proceed to get your book published?
Want to keep all your rights and all your royalties?
Want it to look as good as a Top 10 publisher?
Need help with editing, layout, cover design?
Want it out there selling in 90 days or less?

Visit our website for some exciting new options!

www.chalfant-eckert-publishing.com

www.ingramcontent.com/pod-product-compliance
Lightning Source LLC
Chambersburg PA
CBHW071452070426
42452CB00039B/1139